The Science of a Guitar

The Science of Sound

By Anna Claybourne

Science and Curriculum Consultant:
Debra Voege, M.A., *Science Curriculum Resource Teacher*

Gareth Stevens
Publishing

Please visit our web site at **www.garethstevens.com**.
For a free color catalog describing Gareth Stevens Publishing's list of high-quality books,
call 1-800-542-2595 (USA) or 1-800-387-3178 (Canada). Gareth Stevens Publishing's fax: 1-877-542-2596

Library of Congress Cataloging-in-Publication Data
Claybourne, Anna.
　　　The science of a guitar / by Anna Claybourne.
　　　　　p. cm. — (The science of—)
　　　Includes bibliographical references and index.
　　　ISBN-10: 1-4339-0042-4　　ISBN-13: 978-1-4339-0042-6 (lib. bdg.)
　　　1. Guitar—Acoustics—Juvenile literature.　2. Music—Acoustics and physics—Juvenile literature.
　I. Title.
　　　ML1015.G9C65　　2008
　　　787.87'1922—dc22　　　　　　　　　　　　　　　　　　　　　　　　　2008039918

This North American edition first published in 2009 by
Gareth Stevens Publishing
A Weekly Reader® Company
1 Reader's Digest Road
Pleasantville, NY 10570-7000 USA

This U.S. edition copyright © 2009 by Gareth Stevens, Inc.
Original edition copyright © 2008 by Franklin Watts. First published in Great Britain
in 2008 by Franklin Watts, 338 Euston Road, London NW1 3BH, United Kingdom.

For Discovery Books Limited:
Editor: Rebecca Hunter　　　　Designer: Keith Williams
Illustrator: Stefan Chabluk　　　Photo researcher: Tom Humphrey

Gareth Stevens Executive Managing Editor: Lisa M. Herrington
Gareth Stevens Senior Editor: Barbara Bakowski
Gareth Stevens Creative Director: Lisa Donovan
Gareth Stevens Cover Designer: Keith Plechaty
Gareth Stevens Electronic Production Manager: Paul Bodley
Gareth Stevens Publisher: Keith Garton
Special thanks to Laura Anastasia, Michelle Castro, and Jennifer Ryder-Talbot

Photo credits: Shutterstock, cover; Corbis/Mimmo Jodice, p. 4; istockphoto.com, p. 5; istockphoto.com, p. 6;
Corbis/Fernando Bengoechea/Beateworks, p. 7; Corbis/Gary Houlder, p. 8; istockphoto.com/Joze Pojbic, p. 9;
istockphoto.com/Rob Friedman, p. 11 top; Corbis/Aero Graphics Inc., p. 11 bottom; istockphoto.com/Jose Gil,
p. 13 top; Corbis/Underwood & Underwood, p. 13 bottom; Corbis/Kelly Mooney Photography, p. 14;
istockphoto.com/Roberto A. Sanchez, p. 15; istockphoto.com/Jaimie Duplass, p. 17; Corbis/Neal Preston, p. 18;
istockphoto.com/Ernest Fan, p. 19; istockphoto.com, p. 20; istockphoto.com/Annett Vauteck, p. 21 top;
istockphoto.com/Lisa F. Young, p. 21 bottom; Corbis/Kevin Dodge, p. 22; Corbis/Owen Franken, p. 23;
Corbis/Sylvain Safra/Hemis, p. 24; istockphoto.com, p. 25; istockphoto.com/Nathan McClunie, p. 26;
Corbis/Victor Fraile/Reuters, p. 27; Corbis/Marc Bryan-Brown, p. 28; istockphoto.com/Oleg Prikhodko, p. 29 top;
Getty Images/John MacDougall, p. 29 bottom. Every effort has been made to trace copyright holders. We
apologize for any inadvertent omissions and would be pleased to insert appropriate acknowledgments in a
subsequent edition.

Printed in the United States of America
1 2 3 4 5 6 7 8 9 10 09 08

Contents

Words that appear in **boldface** type are in the glossary on page 30.

What Is a Guitar?

When did you last hear the sound of a guitar? The guitar is featured in a lot of popular music on the radio, on TV, in films, and probably on your iPod! Many people play the guitar and have one at home. How does a guitar work? How does it produce sounds—and turn those sounds into music?

Strings on a Box

A guitar is basically a box with strings attached to it. The strings are played by plucking them, or pulling them gently and then letting go.

People have played instruments similar to guitars for thousands of years. They did not all look like a modern guitar, but they worked in the same way. For example, the ancient Greeks and Romans played a guitar-like instrument called a cithara. In India, people have played sitars for more than 5,000 years.

▼ *This painting from ancient Rome, dating from about 2,000 years ago, shows early stringed instruments.*

Music in Our Lives

Humans have been singing, dancing, and playing instruments for thousands of years. Music can cheer you up, pass the time, inspire you, and help you have fun with others.

You probably hear music often. It seems to be everywhere, from your dentist's office to the supermarket. People sing songs at religious services, at school, and at celebrations.

Try It Yourself

If you have a guitar at home or in your classroom, try some of the activities described in this book. If you do not have a guitar, you can make a simple one by stretching some long rubber bands over an empty tissue box. Pluck the bands to make sounds.

How Sound Works

Music is made of sound, and sound is made by moving air. In this book, you will find out how guitars and other objects make sounds—and sometimes music.

Body

Strings

Neck

*▲ This is a basic **acoustic guitar**. It has six strings attached to a curved, hollow wooden body with a long neck. The player plucks the strings with one hand and presses on them with the other to make different notes.*

Making Sounds

The strumming of a guitar. The crash of a drum. Hands clapping. The rumble of thunder. All those sounds are different, but they are made in the same way. Sound happens when air **vibrates**.

Good Vibrations

When you pluck a single guitar string, it vibrates. The string moves back and forth very quickly. As the string vibrates, it pushes against the air around it. Air, like other substances, is made up of tiny parts called **molecules**. As the vibrating string pushes against the air molecules, it makes them vibrate, too. The vibrations spread out through the air. When they reach your ears, you hear a sound.

String Sounds

Of course, not all strings sound the same. A guitar string sounds very different from a violin string. They sound very different from a string inside a piano. Even on a single guitar, you can make many sounds. The sounds depend on what the string is made of, how long and thick it is, how tightly it is stretched, and how it is played.

String Family

The guitar is just one instrument that uses vibrating strings. Violins

▶ *The vibration of a guitar string makes air vibrate. The vibrations produce sound.*

Speedy Strings

The strings on a musical instrument vibrate quickly to make a sound. If you pluck the E (top) string on a guitar, it vibrates back and forth 330 times a second!

▲ *There are many strings inside a grand piano.*

and cellos have strings, too. You play them by pulling a bow across them. A bow is a wooden rod with fine hairs stretched between its ends.

Did you know that a piano is a stringed instrument, too? When the player presses the keys, felt hammers hit steel strings. The hammers pull back, and the strings continue vibrating. The vibrations are **amplified**, or made louder, by a **soundboard**.

Sound reaches the ear.

Vibrations spread out.

Air molecules move.

A guitar string is plucked.

▲ *Vibrations spread out in the air from a moving guitar string. You cannot see the vibrations, but your ears can sense them.*

Sound All Around

What can you hear right now? If you listen carefully, you are sure to hear something. The sound might be a computer humming, people talking, or your own breathing. All around you, objects are making the air vibrate and producing sounds.

Vibrating Air

Many kinds of objects make sounds by making air vibrate. For example, car engines, washing machines, and lawn mowers are noisy because they vibrate as they work. When you talk, air blows through your throat, making parts of it vibrate to produce sound.

An object does not have to vibrate itself to make air vibrate. When you clap your hands, they don't vibrate. The clapping simply pushes some air. That air pushes against the air next to it, setting up a vibration.

Fade Away

The air around you is rarely still. It is constantly buzzing with sound

▼ *We use clapping to make a loud noise when we applaud a performance.*

vibrations. Unless you have severe **hearing impairment**, it is almost impossible to hear no sound at all. Hearing impairment is complete or partial loss of hearing in one or both ears.

Once a sound has been made, it doesn't stay around forever. After you pluck a guitar string, the vibrations become weaker as they spread out through the air. Finally,

the air stops moving. If the vibrations of air did not stop, all the sounds ever made would still be echoing around the world!

▼ *Noisy machines such as chainsaws make strong sound vibrations that can damage your ears. This logger wears ear protection to help prevent hearing loss.*

A Silent Space

There is one place that is completely quiet—a **vacuum**. A vacuum is a space with nothing in it—no air, water, or other substances. Sound can travel only if there are molecules that can vibrate. In a vacuum, there are no molecules of any kind. There is nothing to vibrate, so sound vibrations cannot spread out.

Ticking clock

Air is pumped out of the jar to create a vacuum.

Glass jar

◄ *In this experiment, a ticking clock is placed inside a jar. Then all the air is pumped out to make a vacuum. The clock keeps working, but the ticking sound stops. Do you know why?*

Waves of Sound

Sound vibrations travel in waves. Imagine throwing a pebble into a pond. Small waves, or ripples, spread out in circles around the spot where the rock hits the water. Sound works the same way. Instead of spreading out across a flat surface, though, **sound waves** spread out through the air in every direction.

How Sound Waves Work

Sound waves are different from waves in water. Water waves make the molecules in water move up and down. Sound waves make the molecules in air move back and forth. In each wave, some of the molecules are pressed tightly together. Some molecules are spaced out. If you could see a sound wave, it would look like the image below.

Air molecules that are squeezed together

Air molecules that are spread out

One sound wave

Sound Is Energy

Sound is a type of **energy**. Energy comes in many forms, such as motion, light, heat, and electricity. All types of energy make something happen or work. Energy cannot be created from nothing, and it cannot be destroyed. It can only change from one form to another.

When you pluck a guitar string, you make it vibrate. This **kinetic energy**, or motion energy, changes into sound energy, in the

◄ *This kind of wave is called a **longitudinal wave**. The molecules vibrate along the direction in which the wave is moving, instead of bobbing up and down like a sea wave.*

▲ A fan who is watching this player from a seat 186 yards (170 meters) away will hear the sound of the bat hitting the ball about a half second after it happens.

form of a sound wave. Where does the sound energy go? As sound waves fade, they change into heat energy. They make the air around them just a bit warmer (but not so much that you can feel it).

▼ **Supersonic** planes can fly faster than the speed of sound. As they fly past, you hear a boom as the sound waves catch up with one another and join together.

Speed of Sound

Sound waves zoom through the air at about 1,130 feet per second (344 m per second) at a temperature of 70° Fahrenheit (21° Celsius). That is fast—much faster than a car or a train could travel. The temperature and the amount of humidity in the air affect the speed at which sound travels.

How You Hear

You pluck a guitar string, and the vibrations spread out as sound waves. When those waves reach your ears, you hear the sound of a guitar. How does that happen? Inside your ears, small parts work together to pick up sound waves and send them as signals to your brain.

In Your Ears

The eardrum is a thin piece of skin inside your ear. It is tightly stretched, like the skin of a drum. As sound waves enter the ear, the moving air molecules bump against the sensitive eardrum. They make the eardrum vibrate.

The eardrum is linked to more parts inside the ear, and they start vibrating, too. Deep inside the ear is the **cochlea**. This snail-shaped part is filled with liquid. The cochlea is also lined with tiny hair cells. When the liquid vibrates, it makes the hair cells move. Signals from the hair cells are sent to **nerves** that lead to the brain. The brain understands the signals as sounds.

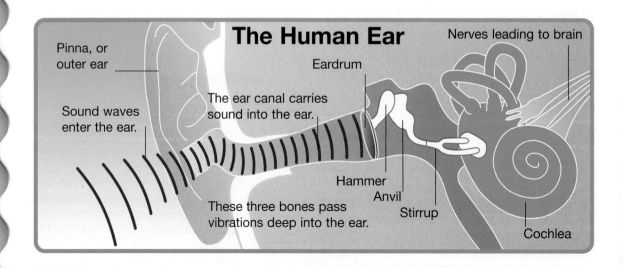

The Human Ear

Pinna, or outer ear

Sound waves enter the ear.

The ear canal carries sound into the ear.

These three bones pass vibrations deep into the ear.

Eardrum

Hammer

Anvil

Stirrup

Nerves leading to brain

Cochlea

▲ *An antelope has large outer ears that catch very faint sounds. The animal's life depends on its ability to hear predators in time to run away.*

Catching Sound

The part of your ear that you can see is the **pinna**, or outer ear. Its shape helps you hear. The pinna's bowl shape catches sound waves and bounces them into your ear, toward the eardrum.

Brain Connection

Your brain plays a big part in hearing. It takes in different patterns of sound and makes sense of them. It can tell whether a sound comes from a guitar, a trumpet, or a piano. It can take the sound of talking, sort it into words, and understand what the words mean.

Your brain can even tell the difference between important sounds and background noise. That's why you can chat easily with a friend in a noisy cafeteria. Your brain listens to the words your friend is saying and tunes out the other sounds.

Feeling Sound

Some people who are unable to hear can sense the vibrations from a musical instrument. The German composer Ludwig van Beethoven (1770–1827) was **deaf** when he created some of his greatest musical works. He held a stick between his teeth and pressed it against his piano. In that way, he could feel the sound vibrations.

Sound in a Box

You know why guitars have strings. What about the big wooden box to which the strings are attached? What does it do? Called the **sound box**, it makes the sound of a guitar richer, deeper, and louder.

Strong Sound

On its own, a vibrating string does not make a loud noise. See for yourself. Stretch a rubber band and pluck it. The sound is soft. Then stretch the rubber band around an empty tissue box. When you pluck the band, it sounds louder.

A guitar works in the same way. The ends of the strings are fixed to the sound box. The sound box has a round hole called the **sound hole**. When you pluck a guitar string, it passes its vibrations into the wood of the sound box. The sound box starts to **resonate**, or vibrate in the same way. The air inside the sound box vibrates, too. This makes a much louder, fuller sound than the string would make by itself. The sound hole lets the vibrations spread out into the air.

◀ *Guitars are built to be strong enough to support the strings. The wood must also be lightweight and flexible enough to resonate well.*

▲ *The sound box of a double bass is similar to the sound box of a guitar. The double bass has two S-shaped sound holes, though.*

That's Intense!

Most musical instruments have a sound box or a part that works like one. For example, violins and cellos have wooden bodies, just as guitars do. Wind instruments have a long, hollow tube with air inside. A drum has a skin with a hollow box-shaped part attached to it.

A Handy Sound Box

You can make your own sound box with your hands. First, sing a few lines of a song. Then cup your hands around your mouth, leaving a small gap. Sing the tune again. It should sound fuller and louder. Why? Air vibrates inside the "sound box" you have made.

Measuring Sound

Some sounds are so quiet, you can hardly hear them. Other sounds, like a thunderclap or a fire alarm, make you cover your ears! What makes a sound loud or quiet?

Turn Up the Volume!

The volume of a sound is its loudness. The higher the volume, the louder the sound that reaches your ears.

Volume depends on the strength of the vibrations a sound makes. If the air vibrates strongly, the molecules move back and forth quickly. They hit your eardrums harder. Your ears sense this as a loud sound. Loud sounds have more energy, so they spread out farther through the air. You can hear loud sounds from a distance.

Quiet or Loud

Try making sounds of different volumes on a guitar. If you pluck a string gently, it vibrates just a bit. It makes the air vibrate gently, so soft vibrations reach your ears. The sound is quiet. If you pluck the string hard, it moves farther and faster, causing bigger vibrations in the air. The sound is louder.

▼ *This diagram shows (1) a gently plucked string and (2) the same string plucked with greater force.*

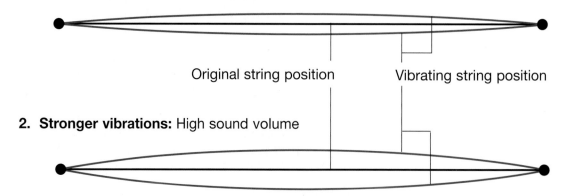

1. **Gentle vibrations:** Low sound volume

Original string position   Vibrating string position

2. **Stronger vibrations:** High sound volume

Measuring Sound

Volume is measured in units called **decibels** (dB). The volume of the quietest sound you can hear, such as very faint breathing, is 10 decibels. There is no upper limit to the decibel scale. The loudest sounds on record measure 80 to 200 decibels. They include big volcanic eruptions and the singing of the blue whale. Scientists have made extremely loud sounds on purpose, in special sound labs.

Protect Your Ears!

Over time, loud sounds can damage your ears and even cause tears in your eardrums. So hear this advice: Avoid listening to very loud music through earphones or earbuds.

▼ *Listening to music is fun, but be sure the volume is not too high. Regularly listening to sounds above 100 decibels for more than one minute can cause permanent hearing loss.*

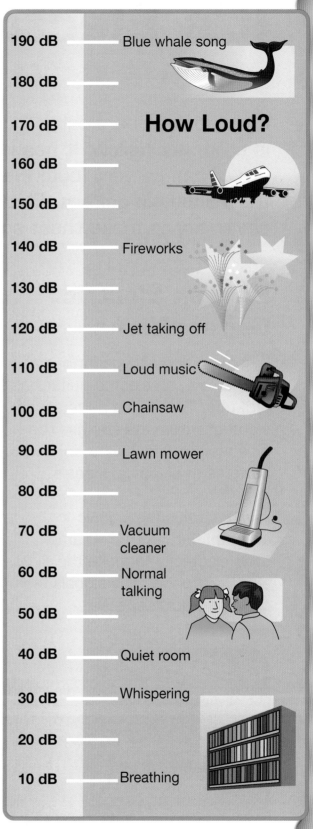

How Loud?

dB	
190 dB	Blue whale song
180 dB	
170 dB	
160 dB	
150 dB	
140 dB	Fireworks
130 dB	
120 dB	Jet taking off
110 dB	Loud music
100 dB	Chainsaw
90 dB	Lawn mower
80 dB	
70 dB	Vacuum cleaner
60 dB	Normal talking
50 dB	
40 dB	Quiet room
30 dB	Whispering
20 dB	
10 dB	Breathing

Source: U.S. Food and Drug Administration

17

It's Electric!

If you look at an electric guitar, you will see that its body is solid, not hollow. It has no sound box. Yet an electric guitar can be very loud! Electric guitars work differently from acoustic guitars. Electric guitars use energy from electricity to make them sound loud.

How an Electric Guitar Works

Where an acoustic guitar has a sound hole, an electric guitar has **pickups**. These little pads sense vibrations from the strings. The pickups turn those vibrations into patterns of electrical signals.

A wire carries the signals to an **amplifier** (amp). The amp uses electricity to make the signals stronger. The signals then go to an electric speaker.

Out of the Speaker

Some amps have a built-in speaker. Others connect to a separate speaker. The speaker turns the electrical signals back into sounds. It uses electricity to make a cone inside the speaker vibrate. This movement makes the air vibrate and creates a sound.

▼ *The sounds from these electric guitars come out of the speakers behind the band.*

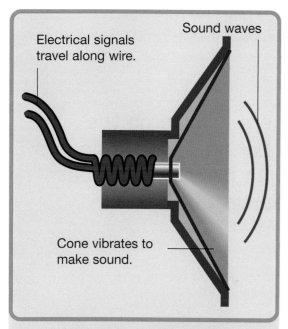

Electrical signals travel along wire.

Sound waves

Cone vibrates to make sound.

▲ *A speaker turns electrical signals into sound waves.*

Amplifying Without Electricity

Before electric amps and speakers were invented, people made sounds louder by using a cone-shaped speaker. When sound enters the narrow end of a cone, the cone resonates and makes the sound louder. Cone-shaped speakers were used for public presentations and on early record players.

Amp It Up

Many other instruments, such as **synthesizers** and electric violins, use electricity. Most instruments can have pickups attached so that their sounds can be amplified and played through a speaker. A **microphone** works like a pickup. People often use microphones to amplify speech or singing.

▶ *This early record player does not use electricity. Its handle is wound to turn the turntable. A metal cone-shaped horn amplifies the sound of the record.*

19

Playing Notes

Guitar players move their fingers around on the strings to play certain notes. For each song, singers sing notes in a specific order. To produce different notes, they must make sound vibrations faster or slower.

Notes on Strings

A guitar has six strings. Each string plays a different note when plucked. The notes are different because the strings are attached to the guitar differently. Some are stretched tighter than others. The tighter a string is stretched, the faster it vibrates. The faster it vibrates, the higher the note it plays. The number of sound waves per second moving through the air is called the frequency. The **pitch** is the highness or lowness of the note.

A guitar player can also play notes on a guitar by pressing a finger on a string, somewhere along the neck. That pressure

▼ *A guitar player can play one note or several different notes at the same time. The player presses his or her fingers against the strings on the neck.*

makes the string shorter. When the player plucks the string, it has a higher pitch. The shorter the string, the higher the note it plays.

In brass instruments, the sound comes from vibrating air inside the tube. Some brass instruments make different notes by making the tube longer or shorter.

Notes have names according to their pitch. The names are the first seven letters of the alphabet: A, B, C, D, E, F, and G.

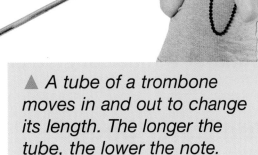

▲ *A tube of a trombone moves in and out to change its length. The longer the tube, the lower the note.*

Voice Pitch

People change the pitch of their voices when they sing. A person sings by taking air into the lungs and breathing it out past the **vocal cords** in the throat. The tighter the vocal cords are stretched, the higher the pitch. The more relaxed the cords, the lower the pitch.

Make a Bottle Organ

You can use glass bottles or jars to make a simple instrument that plays different notes. Collect several identical bottles or jars. Fill them with varying amounts of water. What happens when you tap the bottles or jars with a spoon? They play different notes!

◀ *These singers must hit the right notes with their voices. They do this by using their vocal cords. To lower their voices, they relax their vocal cords, making the cords thicker. To make their voices higher, the singers stretch their vocal cords and make them thinner.*

Sounds Like ...

Even with your eyes closed, you can recognize thousands of sounds. You can tell the slam of a door from the clang of a bell. You can also tell the sound of a flute from the sound of a guitar. What makes the sound of a musical instrument unique?

Quality of Sound

When you play a note on a musical instrument, you do not hear just a single tone. Different parts of the instrument vibrate in different ways, making a series of quieter tones, called **harmonics**.

If you pluck the top string on a guitar, you hear the main vibration as the note E. But you also hear harmonics and other sounds, such as the echoing of the note inside the sound box. This mixture of tones gives the guitar its own special sound, or **timbre**.

Your voice has its own timbre, too, because of the shape of your throat and vocal cords. Timbre helps the ear recognize and identify voices.

Patterns in the Air

Everyday sounds, such as the rumble of a car engine and the song of a bird, have unique sound patterns. Some people can identify different cars or birds just by listening to the sounds they make!

▶ *Even though telephones distort (change) voices, you can probably identify the voices of familiar callers.*

▲ *Some musical instruments are treasured because they have a special sound. This violin was made in Italy by Antonio Stradivari (1644–1737). Stradivarius violins are some of the most expensive musical instruments ever made.*

Amazingly, all sounds are nothing more than patterns of vibrations in the air. The ear senses the way the sound waves move up and down.

of a wave. It shows the patterns of vibrations in a sound wave. Any sound can be represented as a waveform.

Seeing Sound

A sound can be shown as a kind of diagram called a **waveform**. A waveform looks like a drawing

Pure Note

Can you imagine the purest of all sounds? It is a single, steady vibration, with no mixture of other sounds. The noise it makes sounds a bit like a flute.

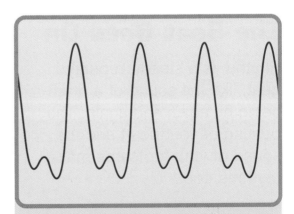

▲ *This waveform represents the sound of a trombone note.*

Making Music

It's hard to say exactly what music is and what makes it different from other sounds. However, most music includes a tune. It has a **rhythm**, or beat. Most pieces of music also have a structure, or shape.

Name That Tune

A tune is a set of notes arranged in an order or a sequence. In most tunes, the notes make a pattern. They may run up and down like steps. A certain series of notes may be repeated. Sing or play a few tunes you know. Can you spot any patterns?

Sometimes, words go along with a tune. Songs are a traditional way of passing information from generation to generation.

The Beat Goes On

Rhythm is a steady, repeated beat, like the sound of a drum being hit again and again. The beating of your heart and the sound of your footsteps make rhythms, too.

Most music has a regular beat. In many songs, the rhythm is played on the drums and the guitar.

Musical Shapes

A piece of music has an overall shape, or structure. For example, a song might have one tune for the verses and a different tune for the chorus. The verses and chorus may repeat throughout the song. Even a simple song such as "Happy Birthday" has its own tune, rhythm, and structure.

▼ *Drummers play at a street carnival in Salvador, Brazil.*

Musical Notation

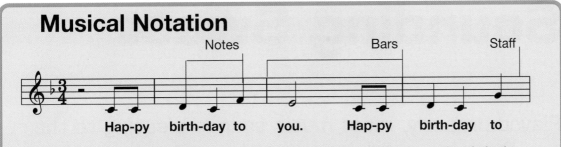

Notes   Bars   Staff

Hap-py birth-day to   you.   Hap-py birth-day to

- The pitch of the note is shown by its placement on the staff. The lower the pitch, the lower the note on the staff.
- Vertical bar lines divide the music into sections of time called measures. In this song, each measure has three beats.

Get It in Writing

Musical notation is a system that represents music as symbols. Notes are arranged on a set of five horizontal lines, called a **staff**. Vertical bar lines divide the piece into groupings of beats, called **measures**. For vocal music, **lyrics** are written below the staff.

▼ *The banjo is a stringed instrument with a wooden body, similar to the guitar. It is often used to play folk music.*

Styles of Music

Music is one of the oldest art forms. Since ancient times, it has been an important part of many cultural and social activities. Various styles of music were popular during different times and in different parts of the world. There are thousands of styles and types of music. They include classical, pop, folk, jazz, blues, rock, and hip-hop.

Sounding Sweet

Played properly, most music sounds pleasing to the ear. But when someone plays the wrong note on an instrument or sings out of tune, you may want to cover your ears! Why do some notes sound wrong and others sound right?

Musical Scales

Most music is written in a particular **key**—a set of tones that sound good together. A **scale** is an ordered set of notes typically used in a key. In the scale of C major, for example, the first note is C. A key includes all of the tones of a particular scale. It also includes all of the **chords** made from those tones. A chord is made up of three or more notes played at the same time.

▼ *A scale has eight notes. The eighth, or top, note—C in this case—is the same as the first note but an **octave** higher.*

Scale of C Major

C D E F G A B C

C D E F G A B C

▲ *You can play a chord by strumming all the guitar strings together.*

▲ *These musicians must all play together, in time and in tune.*

In Harmony

In most music, you don't hear just one note at a time. You hear many notes together. **Harmony** is the combination of musical notes played together as a chord.

Some notes sound good played together. A **consonant** chord sounds pleasing. **Dissonant** chords sound jarring, as if the notes are clashing. Dissonance is sometimes used to create feelings of tension or suspense.

Sounds of Silence

In 1952, American composer John Cage wrote a piece of music called *4'33"* (*Four Minutes Thirty-Three Seconds*). Any number of players can perform the piece on any instrument or instruments. The player does nothing for 4 minutes and 33 seconds! As the musician sits silently, the people in the audience listen to the sounds around them—breathing, passing traffic, an airplane. No two people ever hear *4'33"* the same way!

That's Just Wrong!

In the 20th century, some composers began to experiment with dissonance. They put wrong-sounding notes into their music to shock listeners. They wanted to make their music sound different and new. Austrian-American composer Arnold Schoenberg (1874–1951) and German composer Karlheinz Stockhausen (1928–2007) used dissonance in their music. They influenced the composers and musicians of today.

With the Band

So, you want to be a rock star? You can make great music by yourself or play guitar as part of a group. New technology and music video games even let you rock out with no strings attached!

Battle of the Bands

Most rock bands have at least one guitar player. A typical band is made up of a singer, a lead guitarist, a drummer, and a bass guitarist. A **bass guitar** has four strings instead of six. The bass guitarist usually plays low, deep notes in the background.

Some bands have more musicians and instruments. Others include fewer. Some guitarists, such as B.B. King, perform alone.

In Concert

Bands often play concerts in theaters, music halls, and outdoor concert sites. Thousands of fans gather to enjoy the live music.

Concert sites are specially shaped. They are designed to make sounds bounce to all parts of the space so that the audience can hear. Bands also use electric amplifiers and speakers. A sound engineer controls the sounds coming out of the speakers. The goal is to get a good balance of the different instruments.

◄ *Goo Goo Dolls singer and guitarist Johnny Rzeznik learned to play the instrument when he was in high school. Rzeznik has been a celebrity judge on the reality TV music contest "The Next Great American Band."*

Rock On

No guitar? No problem. Video games such as *Guitar Hero* and *Rock Band* let players rock the house in their living rooms. *Guitar Hero* players score points by using a plastic guitar-shaped game controller to play notes shown on-screen. The playable songs include hits made famous by well-known guitarists Jimi Hendrix and Carlos Santana.

Hands in the Air

Have you ever pretended to be a rock star by playing **air guitar**? Toy makers have tuned in with gadgets that play music when a user strums the air. The toys work by sensing the player's hand and wrist movements.

▲ Most rock bands include a bass guitar. The bass guitar has an extra-long neck and four thick strings instead of six.

Be a Guitar Hero!

Would you like to play music onstage at a live concert? If you don't play an instrument, maybe now is the time to learn! Ask your parents about choosing an instrument and taking lessons. Your school music teacher might have some helpful advice.

▼ *This sound engineer works in a recording studio. He mixes the sounds coming out of the speakers.*

Glossary

acoustic guitar: a basic wooden guitar

air guitar: an imaginary guitar that one pretends to play

amplified: made louder

amplifier: a device that makes electrical sound signals stronger

bass guitar: a stringed instrument designed to play the lower notes in a piece of music

chords: three or more musical notes played at the same time

cochlea: a hollow, coiled tube in the inner ear that plays an important role in hearing

consonant: being in musical agreement or harmony

deaf: unable to hear

decibels (dB): units of measure of the loudness of sound

dissonant: used to describe musical notes that clash

energy: the ability to do work

frequency: the number of sound waves per second

harmonics: quiet sounds that an instrument makes in addition to its fundamental, or main, sound

harmony: two or more notes played together as a chord

hearing impairment: complete or partial loss of the ability to hear

key: a set of musical tones that sound good together

kinetic energy: energy of motion

longitudinal wave: a wave that vibrates in the same direction as it travels

lyrics: the words of a song

measures: regular groupings of musical beats

microphone: a device that collects sound and amplifies it

molecules: tiny particles that make up all matter

nerves: pathways connecting the brain with other parts of the body

octave: the interval between the first and eighth notes of a scale

pickups: devices that sense sound vibrations and turn them into electrical signals

pinna: the part of the outer ear that is visible

pitch: how high or low a sound is

resonate: to vibrate at the same speed as another object

rhythm: the beat of music

scale: a set of musical notes that go up or down by steps

soundboard: a thin wooden board positioned under the strings of an instrument to increase its sound

sound box: a hollow space in a musical instrument

sound hole: the round hole in a guitar

sound waves: waves produced by the vibration of an object

staff: horizontal lines with their spaces on which music is written

supersonic: greater than the speed of sound in air

synthesizers: instruments that create sound electronically

timbre: the distinctive sound of an instrument or a voice

vacuum: an empty space

vibrates: moves to and fro or from side to side

vocal cords: two smooth bands of tissue in the throat that produce vocal sound

waveform: a diagram that shows the patterns of vibrations in a sound wave

Find Out More

NIDCD: Interactive Sound Ruler
www.nidcd.nih.gov/health/education/decibel
Find out how loud is too loud.

NIDCD: Travel Inside the Ear
www.nidcd.nih.gov/health/education/video/travel_vid.htm
Take a video voyage into the human ear.

Science Buddies: Guitar Fundamentals
www.sciencebuddies.org/science-fair-projects/project_ideas/Phys_p053.shtml
Learn the basics about wavelength and frequency.

Index